**THANK YOU
TO ALL THE STREETS ARTISTS
OF CHICAGO**
YOU ARE AN INSPIRATION TO LIFE ITSELF
ALL OF YOU
THANK YOU

**A VERY SPECIAL THANK YOU
TO THE PHOTOGRAPHERS**
especially:
**OSCAR ARRIOLA
CHRIS DIERS
THOMAS FENNELL IV
PATRICK HERSHBERGER**

YOUR GENEROUS SPIRITS
HAVE MADE A REALITY OF A DREAM
YOU HAVE MY MOST DESERVING GRATITUDE
I AM INDEBTED TO YOUR

Chicago Street Art | First Edition
© 2011 Joseph J. Depre. All Rights Reserved
Compiled, Written, Designed, and Edited by: Joseph J. Depre
Some Words by: Oscar Arriola, BonusSaves, Chris Diers, Thomas Fennell IV, Patrick Hershberger, and Tiptoe
Lead Photographers: Oscar Arriola, Chris Diers, Patrick Hershberger, and Thomas Fennell IV
More Photographs by: Will Chambers, Juan Chavez, Cyro, The Grocer, Cody Hudson, MELT, Mental 312,
Ray Noland, Brendan "Solve" Scanlon, Andy Schriver, Sighn, Chris Silva, Elizabeth Slabaugh,
Brittany Steiner, The Viking, and You Are Beautiful
All Photographs are included under nonexclusive licenses from the Photographers.
Copyrights to the Photographs are retained by the Photographers.
ISBN: 978-0-615-46122-9

For my Mom, and the memory of Dad

An Invitation to the Dance

My introduction to Street Art was not so unlike that of many. It stemmed out of a fateful night of restless inspiration with roots in graffiti. My habitually nocturnal lifestyle, combined with the relentless curiosity of youth, and the quest to experience all that city life had to offer, called me into the street during the dark hours of early morning. Unsure of what I would find I gladly opened myself to fate and let it guide me where it may. As luck would have it, a turn style jump onto the CTA Blue line led me to a fortuitous meeting with a graffiti artist that would change my life forever. Unusually trusting of a perfect stranger with a camera, this graffiti artist invited me along for the ride of a lifetime. I can remember the ecstatic thrill and the chill of the early spring breeze on the rooftop he was about to Bomb. The rhythmic hiss of the spray can created the music that was in perfect sync with body as the artist danced along the wall. His dance was highlighted by the strobing lights and the crackles of electric blues sparking from the track of passing el-train cars like some private dance floor designed just for this exclusive masquerade ball whose only invites were the artist, his ego, and the realities of his environment. I was bearing witness to what I could only believe was an expressive art form in line with Jackson Pollack, an evolution of action painting taken to a risky, "get it right the first time," extreme. It was a cross between a graceful fluidity, a playful wrestling match between the artist and his ego and a percussive jab at the world he lived in. But this was not happening on canvass stretched, bound, and hidden within the walls of a studio. This struggle of opposing wills integrated itself into the very environment from which the artist was a product… bricks and grime, tarpaper and cement, noise and the rush of traffic, now quiet, below. The act of painting transformed the environment into a canvass borderless and free, made of life itself. The beauty was overwhelming as the adrenalin pulsed through my veins as I played lookout. I knew. My eyes were seeing for the first time.

Moving through the city was never quite the same after that. The graffiti tag was no longer the visual noise of the urban landscape but a post, marking another soul passing through that space and time. I started noticing them everywhere as letters from friends saying hello, the gestural mark giving some evidence to their state of mind at the moment. Through this observation I started to notice something else as well, a different kind of gesture that was using an entirely different visual vocabulary. This was a vocabulary that was more versatile and adaptive to a communication beyond relentless will and ego. And so, I was introduced to the realm of the Street Artist. Street Art carried the same raw force and urgency of expression as graffiti but had the capability of providing even more freedom to the artist because it was not bound to material, technique, or style. It was free to "reinterpret" formal qualities from art history or attempt the creation of entirely new forms of its own or, at best, discover contemporary forms that were carved from the specific instant the work was created.

This urgency and freedom of message has made Street Art's relationship with the world at large similar to an intensely passionate love affair. Perhaps a forbidden love affair that carries consequence, risk, and that part of the human spirit that refuses to say "NO" to authenticity. It burns with a stellar brightness driven by flames of intense ecstatic emotion filled with nuance, fading as it passes through its ephemeral existence. But in those brief moments of existence it projects the light of the creative human spirit that illuminates the life of city streets, and all of its inhabitance. A single piece of Street Art is capable of expressing a lingering experience out of the mundane routine by providing a smile, or laughter, or empowering intimacy. And it does this all out of chance, purely out of the exuberant happenstance of an unsuspecting passing observer. This is evident in the way Street Art often challenges ideas, defines politics, and adds a unique and profound beauty to the character of the life for those attentive enough, and open enough, to experience the vital force of creativity that is Street Art!

In Chicago, the Street Art milieu is championed by a diverse and dynamic group of individuals who utilize a great number of different techniques and skills to project their subjective perspectives.

Juan "Angel" Chavez, one of the first Street Art practitioners in Chicago, utilized material discarded by fellow urbanites to create elaborate abstract found object sculptures that were both graphic and expressive. Capturing the brilliance of pure imagination, he literally transforms the city into a surreal landscape of play. His actions quickly began to attract and influence the work of other artists drawn to the street. Collaboration was inevitable and he began working with the likes of Mike Genovese, Cody Hudson, and Chris Silva. Each artist brought a different style and skill set to what became elaborate Street Art installation pieces reminiscent of Dada collage and sculpture.

One of the most noted works created by members of this collaborative force was a piece entitled, *Sur Del Cero*, or "*South of Zero*" as it roughly translates into English. This is a prime example of the artists utilizing the very discards of city life as material re-appropriated into gestures expressive of the contemporary urban milieu both through form and content. The installation is the size of an abandoned city lot and is composed of everything from street barricades, to blown up letter fonts that resemble grocery store advertisements, to a foosball table. The work captures the scale of the jumbled, rhythmic, noisy, condensed, and often times chaotic, essence of urban life.

SUR DEL CERO; 2004

Collaborative public installation:
Juan "Angel" Chavez
Mike Genovese
Cody Hudson

JUAN "ANGEL" CHAVEZ

CODY HUDSON

Chris Silva : 1992

CHRIS SILVA

Chris Silva | David Cuesta
Mike Genovese

Chris Silva | Cody Hudson

Chris Silva | Cody Hudson

Chris Silva | David Cuesta

BONUS SAVES

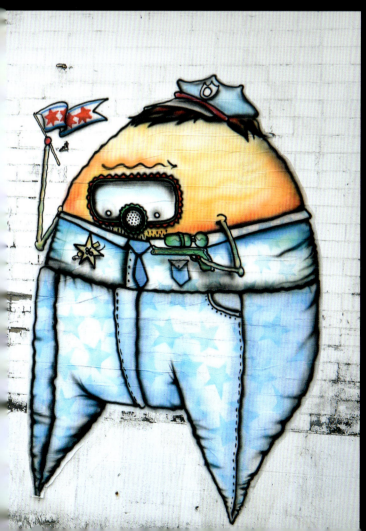

BROOKS GOLDEN • THE SEVENIST

ARTILLERY

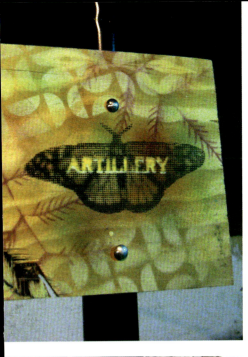

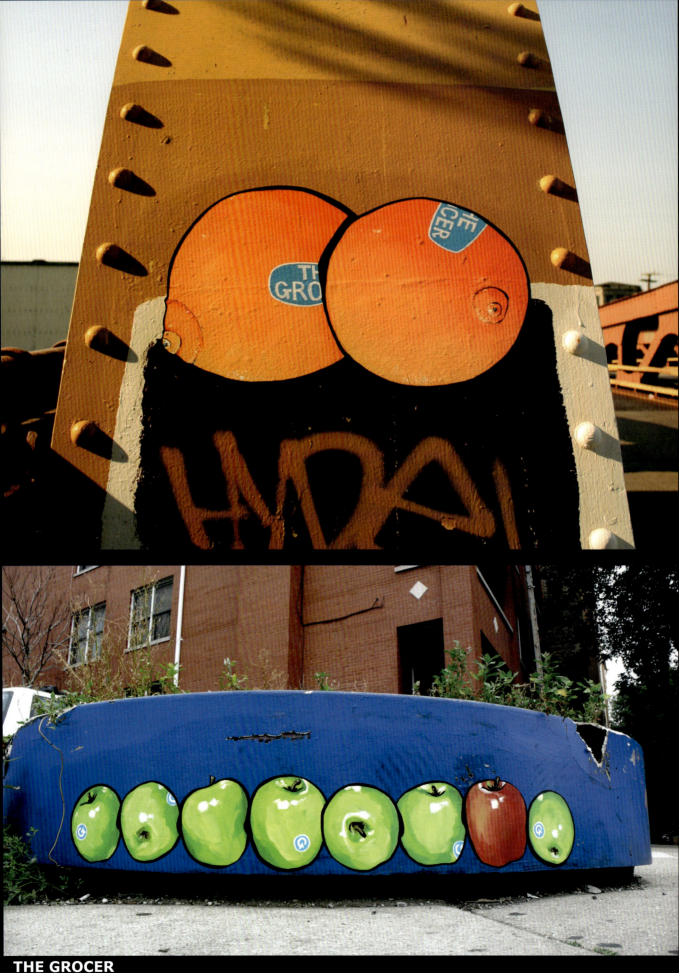

THE GROCER

GOONS

THE VIKING

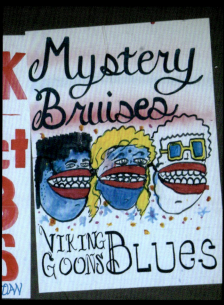

GOONS AND THE VIKING

SONNY RAINCLOUDS

SIGHN

YOU ARE BEAUTIFUL

C L S

TINY

HEBRU BRANTLEY

MELT

CRO

CHOKE

'18 AND COUNTING'

TEWZ

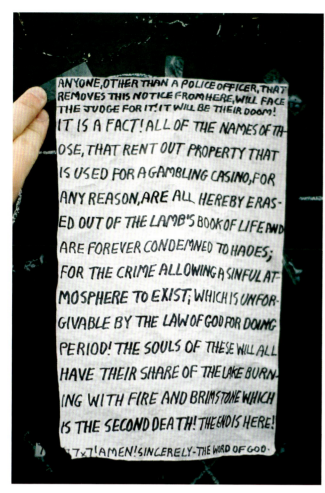
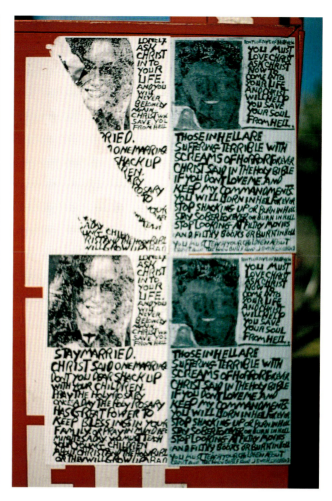

CRAZY TALK / ARTIST UNKNOWN

CYRO

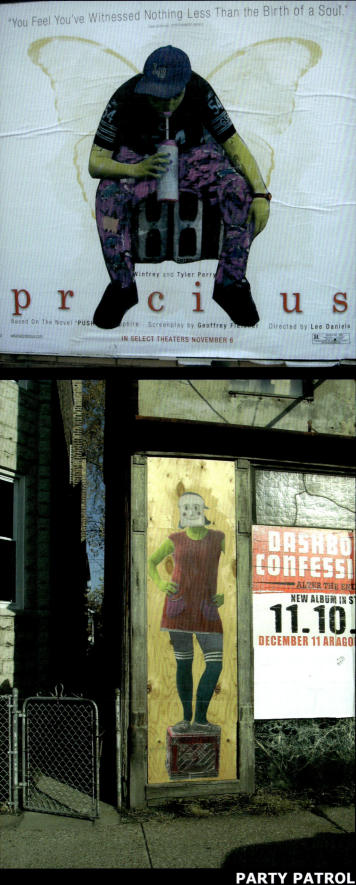

BLÜTT

ARTIST UNKNOWN

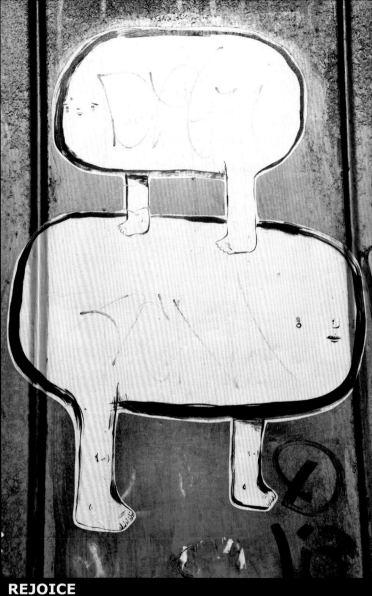

REJOICE

SARO

KLEPTO SALEM

BRENDAN "SOLVE" SCANLON

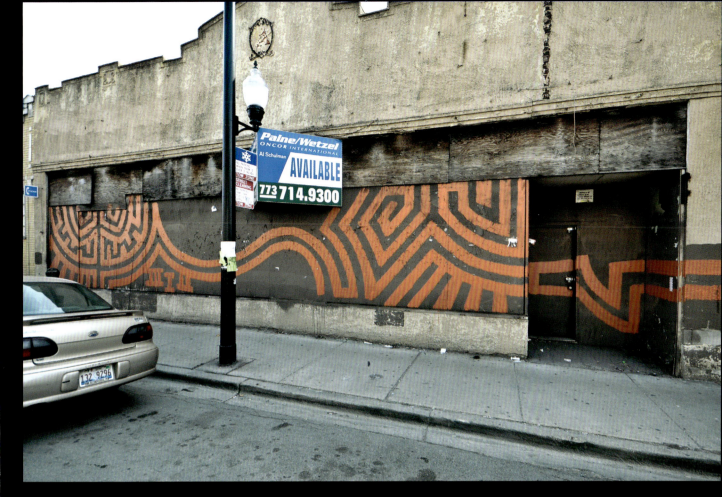

MENTAL 312

SEÑOR CODO

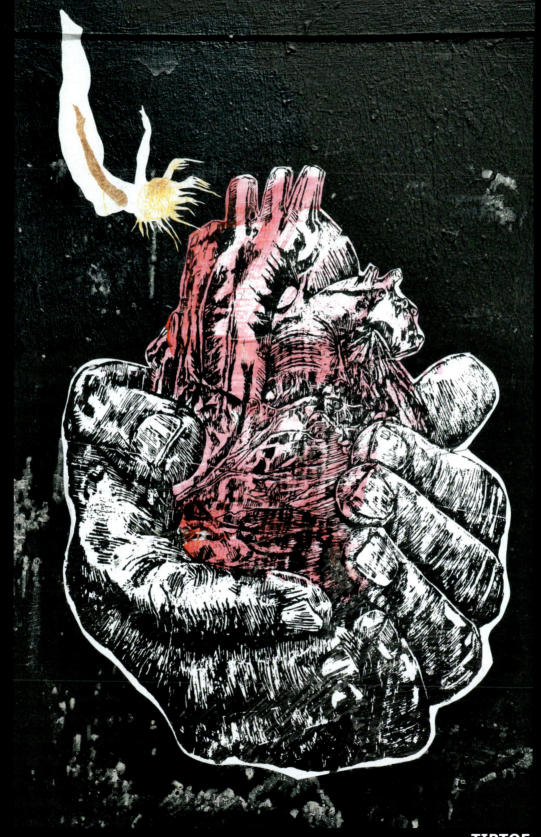

NICK ADAMS

THE BUFF

Love it. Hate it. Respect it.

Every Street Artist knows "the buff" is a force to be reckoned with and here in Chicago it's a fact of life. The upstanding city employees officially known as "Mayor Daley's Graffiti Blasters" are ever vigilant and hold their responsibility to keep the city "beautiful" in the highest regard. While they do employ a number of beautification techniques they are primarily responsible for painting everything in the city the color of excrement. This practice has lead to Chicago's acquisition of the not so endearing nickname BROWNTOWN.

Most Street Artists consider "the buff" to be a State sponsored censorship regime actively suppressing the creative voice of human expression and in doing so preventing the growth of Chicago's fledgling artistic community. So, it is imagined, that if the city would just leave Street Art alone the work would broaden the cities' global recognition in this artistic arena which would then add to the cultural prosperity of the city as a whole.

However, there is a positive side to "the buff". Graffiti Blasters weed out the less "inspired" works, and keep the canvass clean. This is an act that is a great catalyst for expediting artistic development and evolution. But more importantly, "the buff" keeps the observer aware of the fact that the exquisite beauty of human expression won't last. Knowing a spectacular piece of work might be gone as soon as you turn the corner only makes the power of the work burn brighter. Viewing art becomes an experience and not just a passive act.

If only these Graffiti Blasters knew the power they held. I would like to believe that at least a few of these city workers understood the vital force they breathe into the essence of Street Art. But I'm sure to most of them, they are just doing their job. In any case, if you guys are reading this, with all respect, would it hurt to work just a little slower?

IT'S YOURS, TAKE IT!

Everyone these days have heard of flash mobs. They are the seemingly spontaneous appearance of huge numbers of people that come out of nowhere for a specific political, artistic, or social "moment" of solidarity and then are gone. Street artist BonusSaves brilliantly devised a similar spontaneous event he initially called It's Yours, Take It!. Simply put, out of apparently nowhere an installation of artworks appears on an urban street corner. These installations would often be elaborate "exhibitions" of artworks ranging in size, style, and taste depending on the contributing artists. These displays of art were placed on the street in a "freely offered" gesture to the world.

It's Yours, Take It! grew out Bonus' experience as an active practitioner of Free Art Friday and its corresponding Flickr group. Bonus was taken in by the positive effects that Free Art Friday had on both himself and the recipients of his work and decided to escalate the practice into the creation of the more elaborated spontaneous street galleries that became It's Yours, Take It!. Soon the idea was a global phenomenon. Each "gallery" was organized by a local artist from a select city who would collect work from around the world to be displayed in a location of their choosing. There was so much enthusiasm from the street art community that the first It's Yours, Take It! took place simultaneously in Aviv (Israel), Southsea (Hampshire, UK), Chicago, Honolulu, Tempe and Phoenix. Since then, It's Yours, Take It! has popped up in cities the U.S. from New York and Boston to San Francisco and Los Angeles, and has branched out internationally to places like Australia, Brazil, Germany, Ireland, Singapore, and Iran.

The project allows people to make art for the pure joy of creation and to "gift" it with no money involved in the exchange between the creators/exhibitors and the public who take it. Galleries spring up in a location for hours to display their temporary international collection of art. The installation then vanishes from the location leaving only the photographic evidence of its existence. The intent, as a group, is to promote spontaneous sharing and to make people smile. The only form of payment allowed is a photograph of the art's recipient with their new piece of art in hand. These images are uploaded to IYTI's Flickr group where the artists involved and general public can share those moments, continuing the discussion between artist and their work's new owner. You can find all the images and discussions at http://www.flickr.com/groups/itsyourstakeit/

-BonusSaves

DON'T FRET

As I struggle to describe my interest in street art and reasons behind why I choose to document it in photos, I keep coming back to the same sticking point: IT ISN'T ABOUT ME.

I'm not the one doing the hard part; it's the artists who risk their freedom, livelihood, and their neck just to decorate our built environment. But while I can appreciate their work to embellish what's often an otherwise boring urban landscape, there are plenty of people who don't. And even more who seem to go about the business of their day without so much as a glance toward the art that someone took the time to make, display, and share with them. Then of course there are the Mayor's paint-wielding, sandblasting stormtroopers. We should all take a moment to thank them for ensuring the city's alleys, overpasses and abandoned buildings remain a totally disgusting shade of greyish-brown.

Even as I write this, I worry that the artists will think I'm taking too much credit for something they did. Truth be told, with a few exceptions I've never had contact with any of the artists whose art I photograph, and it isn't usually feedback on photos. As a result, I don't know exactly what they think of my documenting their art, but I know it's become a passion of mine to drive, walk and bike off the beaten path to see what of their work I can find. I don't seek clues to discover their identities or catch them in the act, but rather I just exist in this ever-expanding hide-and-seek through the city we both love; they create the art, and I go looking for it. And in doing so, I discover a whole lot of the city I wouldn't have without the art. An afternoon drive with the windows down, bouncing down the back alleys of the West Loop or Wicker Park, double parking and sticking a camera lens out the window—that's my 'Saturday at the gallery.'

I made my 'rookie mistakes,' like asking too many questions in an internet forum, which drew accusations of being a cop, or posting too many details about a piece's location and feeling partially responsible for its early demise. That feeling, in particular, is a lot like knocking over a vase at a dinner party. I was just here to enjoy the art and share it with people, and I might've helped turn the wrong people on to the spot, and it got torn down. But a funny thing happened when I started to shoot more photos of street art and got better at it: an unsigned message came in, suggesting I look and see what I'd find down a certain alley. And sure enough, a fresh piece hung there that I hadn't seen shared anywhere yet. So who was it that wanted me to see it? I still don't know, but I appreciated the note. I got the feeling at least someone dug what I was up to, and the feeling was certainly mutual. The comments that the shot received were mostly about the new piece, and a few about what a cool find it was. But to me, it was admission into a sort of ecosystem that's created between these artists, the public that wanders past without looking, other people who are genuinely interested in the art, and photographers like me who show our appreciation by documenting and sharing what we see.

So while I appreciate the attention on my photos, you should know I'm also totally uncomfortable about it—I just do my best to capture a scene, either to document the artist's piece or to show you, the viewer, how the world around it seemed to be reacting. These guys (and gals) deserve all the credit in the world—without them, I wouldn't be able to make the photos I like so much, and this city would be a much uglier place.

-Thomas Fennell IV

NICE-ONE

"This is the only time Nice-One ever tipped me off to a piece he did. I went that day. By the following day it had been buffed..."

-CHRIS DIERS

    Nobody seems to know who put up the animal cutouts. I witnessed the goose, owl, a couple other birds, wolf, and rabbits. Not only did the original colors merge thoughtfully well with their walls, but the buff felt almost intentional as it sloppily splashed across the pieces. The white rabbits placed on white fence boards were some of the most difficult to spot-if not the outline spray it blended completely with the wall. The wolf appeared to walk and take on the appearance of whatever paint splashed closest to him. The goose flies through the buff only sparing a few white feathers to show through the brown. Without saying anything this Street Art speak volumes of the human traffic walking past those wooden animals. Are we disguising ourselves to hide from our transgressors? Or do some wait to pounce at the first moving shadow? Maybe we just need to fly away from our problems. Or fly right into them.

-PATRICK HERSHBERGER

"Encountering street art is always a happy surprise. It makes you think about the city in a different way. I find myself scanning doorways or newspaper boxes wherever I go; because you never know where a great drawing or tag is going to appear. And when a piece of art appears in an odd spot or is made of some unusual material it makes the experience even better.

Rejoice's lil' hand drawn heads were always fun to find. Then they started getting bigger and appearing in piles and other configurations. Which culminated in this huge head drawing that I photographed in Chicago's Bronzeville neighborhood. I was blown away by both its size and location. You could see it from a block away and it was in an area that doesn't usually have any street art at all. I was on my way to install an art show that morning and seeing that huge drawing in the street really made my day."

-OSCAR ARRIOLA

REJOICE

The Intimacy of Exhibitionism
(an honest paradox)

There are some strange realities in the realm of the Street Artist. Since the beginning of its history, when Street Art began its transition from its roots in graffiti, a fair amount of Street Art has primarily been a projection of elements borrowed from graphic "POP" design. However, there is a certain archetypal Street Artist whose creative endeavors express unique, underlying, esoteric communications of intimate truths. Granted, at first glace the street seems to be a forum counter-intuitive and unreasonable for the artist to divulge their secrets, especially when the communication exposes the piercing realities of human intimacies with such intensity. So why has the street corner and back alley wall become the confessional of choice for this band of misfits, hooligans, rebels, and masked intellectuals?

Consider for a moment that the motivation for a certain breed of Street Artist is not the quest for fame or fortune but the mask of anonymity provided by the street itself. Then the answer to the question, "why the street?" becomes congruent with the question "why the mask?" Sure the immediate simple response to the question is the artist needs to protect him/herself from the illegalities of the act itself, but this is a secondary consequence that is relevant only after the impulse to act. The truth is, there are bigger things to protect oneself from than the police. The mask is a construct, provided by the impersonality of the street, unbound by the rules and responsibilities defined by "respectable" social life. It allows the artist to control a hyper-reality created through a manifested persona. Donning the mask allows the Street Artist to be direct and honest without fear of consequence, judgment, social recourse, or pretention. These vandals are poets whose veils free them from the rules governing the "polite" social reality. In this freedom, the Street Artist expresses pure inspiration unadulterated by the world at large. A world where the truth is dangerous and honesty is a weakness to be exploited. Untruths simultaneously become a virtue that is rewarded, and the cold walls of isolation, imprisoning their own architect. This creates a social reality where words are un-trustable and truths get buried deep, far from the conscious mind.

Masked by the street, the Street Artist is liberated from these dark cells of isolation. This rare variety of artist turns an ethic of selfish desire and conquest upon itself. To this breed honesty is no longer a weakness to be exploited, but the empowering force that binds humanity itself. The Street Artist transforms the street into a sacred realm of ritualistic expression and self-reclamation. The liberated form of expression on the street can be trusted because there is no ulterior motive. It is free of the influence of commerce, the universal solvent of truth. There is nothing to be gained other than true voice. And once this truth is expressed through action it becomes familiar. It prompts a contagious response. It creates a conversation through direct action. These communications are one of the purist forms of expression left in this isolating social structure. They are an exhibition of the most intimate aspects of humanity, unbound by, yet completely immersed in, society.

Joseph J. Depre

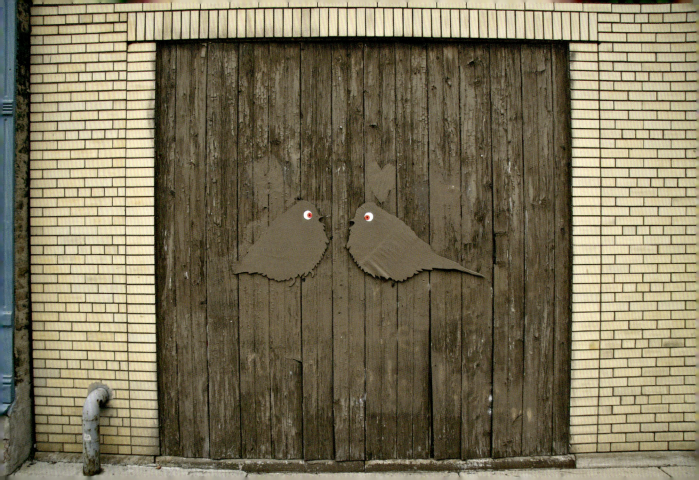

The
Ephemeral Nature
of the Absolute Truth

Joseph J. Depre

Perhaps you're thinking right now, "wow, what an impressive title, but can it deliver a satisfying premise?" Let's hope I can address this question and put the surrounding concerns in context within the immediate confines of a limited time and space. If you would, indulge me for a moment. Let's take some time to think about the nature of experience itself. In fact let's keep it simple and limit our thoughts to empirical experience.

And so, picture this: your mother's embrace... the play of childhood... that first kiss... your first pay check... moving out from under your parents roof... your first high... the ever powerful orgasm... your first fight... the loss of a close friend... the first time someone screwed you over just because they could... finding yourself face down in the mud... seeing a hand extended to pull you out... the first time you really understood something... the first time you felt really understood.

Obviously, in "normal" human behavior there are natural, even predictable, reactions to these events and experiences, be it love... arousal... accomplishment... freedom... wonder... ecstasy... rage... shock... frustration... depression... humility... rebellion... connection.

Of course all these things have been cataloged in memory and most can often be called up to the forefront of the mind at will, although in varying degree of completeness or accuracy. It is logical that the collection of every preceding experience is fundamentally and absolutely responsible for a person's *Being*; this is true both physically and psychologically, as it affects perception, processes, and combines every preceding experience. One must appreciate the relationship we have to these

moments fundamentally changes as memories slide out of the forefront of our mind and dissipate into residual remembrance.

All this to say, each of us have felt these things, and the continuously dissipating relationship with them will be ever present, ingrained somewhere in the recesses of the mind. While it is impossible to hold all of these moments in the conscious mind simultaneously they do affect the minute-by-minute experiences that define the present. We connect, disconnect, and reconnect constantly with each of them. Every passing moment changes perception, understanding, and consequently the truth of what one is. Think about that song or painting that you couldn't live without only a few years ago. Remember how you would defend it to the death? Whereas you are completely indifferent to, if not annoyed with, it now. Then there was that idea that you believed in so fundamentally that it seemed to control every aspect of your personality, and now, it's a foolish thing to you. Oh... how our worlds used to be so flat. This is a human state of *Being*, active in the world with an open heart and mind. Why shouldn't it be this way? How else could one grow, adapt, and evolve, if not by excepting every experience for what it is, processing it while moving through it, and then letting it fade into time. And fade it must. It is impossible to solidify the past, for time is the adjuster of memory.

Longing for re-created past moments produces nostalgia and closes one off to new joys. Dwelling on previous injustices provides no relief. These things are facades, self-imposed false realities. In fact, past events or insults often get conflated or exaggerated in the mind, becoming as destructive as a junkie, chasing the elusive dragon of the first high. The moment has passed, never to return, even as it resonates in memory, it dissolves.

The same is true in the physical world. Even the brightest star shining in the galaxy will die in a great explosion casting out an intensely overwhelming light. Ever so briefly, it will consume everything in its immediate proximity and then dissolve into the universe as it passes through time and space. It will always *Be*, progressively resonating away from its origin, growing fainter, having a smaller and smaller effect on things farther from it until it is all but completely un-recognizable. Likewise, the most profound and intense events in life are experienced only briefly and will resonate in the mind and dissolve into memory as time carries it away from the immediate proximity of the event and new experiences become superimpose. It is inevitable that one will eventually forget the event as an absolute, remembering only the memory of the memory as a memory that has very little basis in the reality from which it came.

Historical catalog, as a model of collective memory, works in a similar way. It provides a sense of greater understanding in that it expands beyond the subjective experience of the individual and enters into a more generalized space of *collective-subjectivity*. This is a collection of a multitude of singular perspectives, or a catalog of a general overview of events that individuals experience as a group. The history of World War II can be told as a series of generalized sequential events but each individual on the planet experienced those events from their personal perspective. From those who landed on the beaches of Normandy, to the sailors at Pearl Harbor, the fiancés left on the home front, witnesses of death or news of death, to the prisoners in the camps of Germany, Russia, and the U.S., to the Londoners experiencing the blitz, to the Berliners living in Germany, each has a remembrance that was their experience.

While there are Historians who try to catalog History in fine detail, there are also those who omit, commit, and manipulate historical "fact" to suit external or internal agendas. This is NOT to say that History is irrelevant or should be disregarded or distrusted. Quite the contrary, History is of the utmost importance. But it is to say that History can never be archived completely and therefore can never be taken as an absolute. There is a popular expression that, "History is written by the Victor," or, "… the Champion." This singular perspective is exclusive and fundamentally incomplete and a wider spectrum of viewpoints is necessary to grasp a greater understanding of past realities. But even with expanded understanding, where each historical catalog is accepted with equality, there are still pieces missing because much of an *alternative-history* or *revisionist-history* is educated-guess work, done by people who did not live through those periods. It must be acknowledged there will always be a variable of misunderstanding or misinterpretation of events.

Life is messy and so are the lives whom make up the fabric of any event in time. It is no different in the current moment. Every Observation, interpretation, perspective, will color the way a person moves through their historical moment contributing to the historical memory bank. It becomes the individual's responsibility to both live in the *Now* and reprocess the past from all newly offered perspectives. What one cannot do.., is relive the past. While the effects of History always remain relevant, because those events brought us to the current moment, the current situation is different in the flow of time. History never actually repeats itself *in the absolute.*

There is only freedom in release, raising the anchor and letting the tide of time carry the individual wherever it may. This is not to say, there should be no effort on the part of each of History's participants. Active response, communication, and unity are necessary as a means of survival in the ever-changing environment of this complex world. These are quintessential tools in obtaining the broader perspective imperative to navigating the collective to more productive currents in the torrent of time. For this navigation to be productive every individual must open him or herself to true communication and connection through the truth. Regardless of the associated feeling, truth is relative and subjective to the

perspective of the individual, and it is important to keep in mind what is true *Now* will not always be true. Even the effects of the most monumental or momentous event of a lifetime will dissolve, as the changing tide will erode even *The Heaviest Stone* into the sand of future beaches.

Is it not the Artist's very job to understand these things? Do their lives not line up with the same model of memory and History as rendered through the premise outlined above? Are they not connected to the effects of time like the rest of us? Yes, the artist is all too human, no higher or lower in the spectrum of humanity. Contrary to the popular projected mythos, the artist is not a solitary individual. They are connected, as we all are, through the collective experience of life. In fact artistic expression through music, poetry, and mythos, acts as the very conduit that binds humanity together.

As with everyone, the experience of the artist, and by extension the expression of, is tiered to the Subjective: of being human; of being Western; of being American; of being East or West Coast; of being north or south side; of class; of social ideological identification; of gender; of ethnicity; of religion; of generation; of the individual, and importantly, of the individual's understanding of history. The more of these subjective categories fall in parallel between the artist and the active observer, the clearer the intent of the artist's expression will be. However, because of the infinite variables of experience, true connection can never be made. Even as a viewer who approaches the work, with the empathy of an open mind and feels connection, has to question if this feeling is merely their own projection. Either way the likelihood of paralleling connection is never more possible than in the immediate of time and space of the manifested expression, the moment of artistic genesis.

It is true, the artist is capable of exploding upon a particular historical milieu with a stellar brightness that both exposes and consumes all things in its immediate cultural vicinity. However, the resonance of even the most explosively powerful masterpiece, aesthetic breakthrough, or understanding fades with every passing generation. As time and space carry the artist away for the moment of their creation, it will redefine the artist's subjective understanding. It is probable if not inevitable, that the masterworks of artistic expression will no longer reflect the specific vitality of the artist. For like everything else, the artist is ever changing, ever adapting to the ebb and flow of the tide of experience, culture, politics, the world, and the universe.

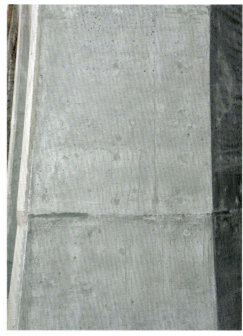

Preserving, archiving, and solidifying the artist's manifested expression separates the work from a cultural context, a context future viewers will never be able to understand or remember in the same absolute way. The only thing framed in "preservation" is a recorded lineage illustrating previous use of method and intent. More often the agenda of the archive is to establish a doctrine of expression categorized into "schools" or "movements." This categorization creates a dangerous imposition of influence upon future creative expression. It is an attempt to define what is un-definable. It is an especially detrimental influence upon artists who follow in suit. It prevents the fluidity necessary to adapt in the contemporary cultural milieu, and impedes the evolution of language, idea, and expression.

In order to break free of the practice of institutional archive and establish a greater understanding of the contemporary moment in culture, there is a need for a critical mass of people working in a creative paradigm that parallels the ephemeral nature of reality. This would be a model of continual adaptation and evolution with the fluidity necessary to respond to the flux of the contemporary cultural environment. It would require release from the structured expectation of established creative paradigms. In doing so, create an alternate approach.

A new kind of art model is required, one open to active communication and barrier-free participation. Establishing a forum for creative expression un-tethered from commerce and its consequential solidification, judgment, objectification, and ownership. Art that equally reflects every possible perspective and nuance of the contemporary cultural milieu. An art-form that is not just a reflection or projection from the Art World but of the people of Society itself.

Of all the creative cultural models currently conceived, Street Art, *in its ideal form,* is the most suited for this freedom. Here is a creative paradigm that has no prerequisite, and is open to anyone who cares enough to participate. It is absent of any excluding intermediary, such as a gallery or a critic. It is a direct communication with the world. It is expressive freedom not limited to style, form, message, or method. It is a paradigm that simultaneously represents artists inspired by every emotive and corresponding style of the contemporary social structure. This includes those who make Street Art for capitalistic aspirations, collectivists, hobbyists, those driven by emotional expression, theoretical or conceptual idealists, or any combination of these. The Street is a level playing field, an equal opportunist beyond the concept of good or bad. The responsibility of judgment is placed solely upon those who choose to acknowledge it… to experience it.

More importantly it is a creative paradigm that is literally integrated into the contemporary environment both physically and culturally. *Viewed as a whole* it allows for a more comprehensive understanding of the immediate cultural milieu. Depending on range of perspectives, this can be understood globally, or specific to individual cities, through the works' particular local dialect. Released into the street, and its corresponding ephemeral fate, the work remains true to both the artist's intent and fleeting subjective reality, allowing the artist and culture to adapt without anchor. Street Art not only concedes to but embraces the ultimate inevitability. It therefore becomes more than just an object *from* a culture incompletely preserved in a glass box, but something that *IS*; a cultural manifestation that exists as an experience within a culture, open to intimate relationship, conversation, and active response. It is alive in the street, and like every experience of life, it will pass into a forgotten time. But in those brief moments, it can burn brilliantly with beauty, illuminate a cultural milieu, and consume the minds of the populous, before it dissolves, making room for the next creative star to explode upon the consciousness.

TIPTOE
'The Heaviest Stone to Carry'

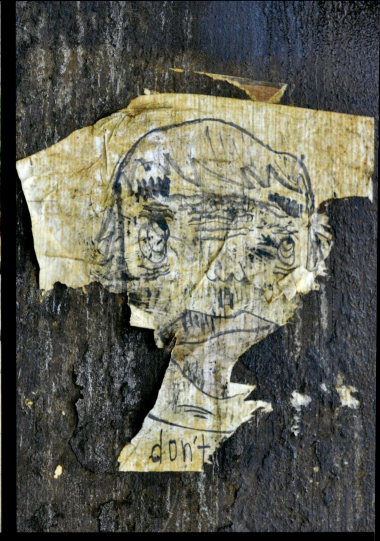

DON'T FRET

GOONS

The Culture of Cool: A Fast, Hard Drop Baby
Banksy's Secret Revolution

Joseph J. Depre

"The spirit of the revolution soared over the land[1]. A tremendous, mysterious process was taking place in countless hearts. The individual personality, having hardly had time to become conscious of itself, dissolved in the mass, and the mass itself became dissolved in the revolutionary élan.[i]"

–the preface to The Battleship Potemkin.

Most people walking in the urban landscape hardly glance at the art on the walls. Like the ubiquitous advertising surrounding the casual pedestrian, Street Art seems to be delivering only a sound bite or a quick shot of eye candy. Banksy, with his piece in Chicago, has proven that there is a great deal of wealth to be found in prolonged in-depth contemplation of Street Art in context of the history of art and the world at large.

The agenda of Postmodern Art, as fundamentally practiced and championed by Andy Warhol, demands that the artist subtract meaning from content. Warhol pushed this idea as a strategy by endlessly reproducing iconic images until they could no longer be linked to their historical realities. Absent of their historical relevance these "stripped naked" icons became significant only as their material being. In the contemporary world this model has been reproduced so often that it has affected the norm of understanding. It has created a thread in the social consciousness that is in line with amnesia. When we are constantly bombarded with "POP" images that deliberately isolate iconic signifiers from their historical context, how could one blame another for not looking beyond the material surface? Indeed, trying to contextualize every image one sees would create a mental riff, if not a cultural psychopathology. This is due to fact that most of these signifiers would be reassembled in a way so far removed from their original context that it would be impossible to make any logical connection at all. In fact, this surface level acceptance has become so normalized that we, as a culture, have all but stopped looking beyond it. But every once in a while there comes an artist that breaks with this pattern of zeros, and deliberately inter-texturalizes historical linkage as a feature of their aesthetic effect. The Banksy stencil in Chicago is one of these profound pieces. Each histori-cal linkage to this piece, through its signifier, reveals an ever-increasing complex realization to the artist's purpose and intent, not only in Chicago, but elsewhere. In order to understand the signifier's inter-textural historical links, one must understand its contextual present.

Chicago has the most notoriously aggressive, authoritarian and governmentally sanctioned censorship in the United States. Well, at least when it comes to Street Art. The fact is, Chicago has some of the harshest anti-graffiti legislation on the books. Penal sentences for those caught in the act of creating Graffiti/Street Art, even for first offenders it can mean weeks, months, or years in jail. This is combined with the relentless censorship machine know as The Graffiti Blasters. The Buff, as The Graffiti Blasters are commonly referred to by the local artists, relentlessly seeks out and destroys all efforts creatively expressed or designed by the Chicago Street Art Community. This systematic "buffing," which primarily means painting everything in the city the color of excrement, is considered, by some, to be the primary reason why Chicago is rarely considered in the global Street Art conversation. Works by international globe-trotting Street Artist stars rarely appear in Chicago. In fact, when the piece by the notorious Banksy arrived in Chicago, during his US tour to promote his film, *Exit Through the Gift Shop*, many were skeptical if it was authentically his.

For those who are unfamiliar with the subject at hand, Banksy simply sprayed a single-layer stencil of a baby carriage onto a wall. His execution of this piece eloquently utilized the discoloring on a wall, outlining a staircase previously removed. His application of the stencil gave the perception of a baby carriage tumbling down the steps. This vandalistic deed is simple enough as far as the act itself is concerned, and admittedly the material surface is "cool," but the complexity of content delivered through the image's historical lineage is masterfully hyperbolic. It reveals his understanding of Street Art, Chicago history, the seminal importance of cinema as a tool in culture and his intent with the subject of his own film.

Considering this is Chicago, and the signifier is a carriage tumbling down a staircase, the first historical link moving backwards along the timeline is Brian De Palma's 1987 film, *The Untouchables*. The film is about government officers going after Al Capone and the Chicago mob. There is a scene in the film in which a baby in carriage tumbles down the steps of Chicago's Union Station. This happens during a shootout between the officers and the Chicago mob. It is also easy to see how Banksy is comparing The Buff's systematic removal of Chicago Graffiti/Street Art to the government officers portrayed in the film. Interestingly enough, in the scene the government officers save the baby in the carriage from harm while simultaneously shooting and killing a group of Chicago mobsters. It has now been months since Banksy's carriage has appeared in Chicago and it is still there, spared/saved by the Chicago authorities (though "vandalized" or riffed upon by other Street Artists). While Banksy may have been commodified by City Hall because of his fame, the powers that be are still relentlessly destroying "the mob" that is Chicago-based Street Art/ists. The Buff has also, in its efforts to eradicate Street Art, destroyed private property and "permission walls" throughout the city without the owner's consent or recourse. Making The Buff a bit "untouchable" in its own right.

But the design of Banksy's carriage more closely resembles the carriage from another film entirely, one in

The Battleship Potemkin; 1925

which *The Untouchables* referenced in homage. This design aesthetic decision by Banksy leads us to the next historical reality of his carriage and another layer of understanding offered through its linkage to Eisenstein's 1925 film, *The Battleship Potemkin*: and *The Odessa Staircase Sequence.*

In some academic circles *The Battleship Potemkin* is known for being the greatest propaganda film of all time. The film is a modified telling of a mutiny aboard the Battleship Potemkin and the corresponding events during the failed Russian Revolution of 1905. These are the events that Lenin credited for being one of the inspirations for the 1917 Russian Revolution which ultimately overthrew the Tsar and lead to the formation of the Soviet Union. The film, itself, was held in the greatest esteem for capturing the essence of the revolution. Street Art's revolutionary essence, and its influence to the history of propaganda, link the two in a common thread already.

But there are more enigmatic links to Banksy's carriage to be found in comparing it to the film's content and style. The content, both in subject matter and representation, has an obvious relationship to Banksy's stencil. Take, for example, the links between the inter-texts/titles of the first five minutes of *The Battleship Potemkin* and the revolutionary spirit at the foundation of the Street Art movement. The Kino translation of the film opens with a preface of a social consciousness of the revolution in Russia.

"The spirit of the revolution soared over the Russian land. A tremendous, mysterious process was taking place in countless hearts. The individual personality, having hardly had time to become conscious of itself, dissolved in the mass, and the mass itself became dissolved in the revolutionary élan." [ii]

If this quote is made non-specific to Russia, and is applied in a general way, it creates a poetic understanding of the social consciousness at the beginning of any revolution, including the newly forming social consciousness of the Street Art Movement. Banksy could also be addressing Chicago by taking the voice of Vakulinchuck in saying:

"Comrades! The time has come when we too must speak out. Why wait? All of Russia has risen! Are we to be the Last?" [iii]

> **"Comrades! The time has come when we too must speak out. Why wait? All of Russia has risen! Are we to be the last?"**

In doing so he might be attempting to inspire more artists in Chicago to join the rebellion that is the International Street Art Movement. Though the piece most relevantly leads to the suggestion that Banksy is comparing the massacres of those who join the Revolution in Odessa to the malicious destruction of Street Art/ists in Chicago. This link can be made in the scene were the carriage appears.

For those who are unfamiliar with this section of the historical reenactment, it begins with the citizens of Odessa providing supplies to the mutinous sailors of The Battleship Potemkin. Then everyone in town decides to enjoy their revolutionary charity by basking in the sun on this enormous staircase. The Tsar's military shows up at the top of the steps and starts shooting the unsuspecting citizens of Odessa as they march down the stairway. No one is spared and the steps become littered with men, women, and children alike. A mother trying to shield her baby in its carriage is shot. The carriage teeters and is sent racing down the steps delivering the child to its doom by the soldier's brutal sword. Anyone who sees this rightfully becomes horrified by the actions of the Tsar's authoritative regime. It is true that the Tsar killed many people in Odessa. In the reality of historical events however, the carriage never fell down the steps of Odessa during a massacre because there was no massacre on the steps of Odessa. There is only the massacre on the steps of Odessa as imagined through Eisenstein's lens and only comes into the social consciousness through the action of making his film.

This bit of information exposes the carriage's most enigmatic inter-textural link to the style of Eisenstein, a link that makes the "carriage and steps" a symbol of a purposed-lie, untruth, a conjured reality, or at the very least a manipulated truism. Eisenstein purposely manipulated his retelling of the events with the intent of eliciting the greatest emotional connection between his audience and the spirit of the revolution in Russia. Eisenstein was so successful in his propaganda that the actual history of the events have been forgotten in the social consciousness and replaced with Eisenstein's façade. Even considering the access to information in 1925, this is still an impressive feat. In light of the reference to the manipulation of historical fact, might it be safe to question whether Banksy actually did the vandalistic deed himself? Indeed he would only need the appearance to have done it to ignite emotional response from his audience. But say, for the sake of argument, we accept that it was Banksy, himself, who actually sprayed the stencil. What are we to take from this message that he has left us?

Considering the timing of the vandalistic act coincided with the opening of *Exit Through the Gift Shop* and the position *The Battleship Potemkin* holds at the foundation of film history, it can be discerned that the two are linked. Following this line of reasoning, one sees that Banksy's nod to Eisenstein could reveal the purpose and intention of his own film, *Exit Through the Gift Shop*, and what the film might really be saying about Street Art. In the age of the Internet, and the readied access to information at our fingertips, the manipulation of historical realities might be thought of as impossible. Even as Wikileaks is exposing embarrassing information about governments all over the world, what does anyone really know about the secretive world of Street Art, the Street Artists, and more specifically about Banksy and his friend Mister Brainwash? The level of ignorance about the historical facts allows a liberty to be taken with the truth. Eisenstein's film became accepted as truth in many places in the world because of levels of public illiteracy and the minimal access to information at the beginning of the Twentieth Century. One has to accept that Banksy's film could be a similar type of historical manipulation due to the limited access to information of historical facts about Banksy, Mr. Brainwash, and the Street Art movement as a whole. Let's start with what is known.

There is the obvious fact that Street Art does exist. A walk down the block in almost any major metropolitan city would reveal this. And, there is a collection of art, dating back years both on and off the street, that has been assembled under the moniker Banksy. There is no doubt that some of the documentary footage provided by Thierry, for *Exit Through the Gift Shop*, are recordings of actual "unscripted" history, captured without conjured purpose or intent. The footage of Thierry meeting Shepard Fairy for the first time and moments where Thierry is following various Street Artists around can be taken as examples of this. This is similar

> **"so then these famous auction houses... all of a sudden they were selling Street Art and everything was going a bit crazy... and suddenly it became all about the money... But it never was about the money."**

to Eisenstein, whose film was based on an actual revolution and whose characters were based on actual people, who participated in that revolution. There is a foundation of truth in the narrative history. All the best lies are based in truth. In order to find out what the manipulated truth is in *Exit Through the Gift Shop* one has to link the signifiers between the two films.

Banksy could have chosen any number of graphic signifiers from The Battleship Potemkin to link his film to the revolution or the history of propaganda. In fact a red victory flag high on a mast would have been a more direct link to the revolutionary spirit. The fact that he has isolated the carriage as the iconic representation of his stencil directly links it to the specific subject in Eisenstein's film that has no actual historical base in reality, or if it did it's a heavily manipulated reality. The "carriage and steps" only come into being solely through the imagination of Eisenstein and the production of his film. Therefore, we have to consider that the subject in Banksy's own film has no actual historical reality, or a heavily manipulated reality that only came into being through the imagination of Banksy. So what is the subject of *Exit Through the Gift Shop*? It is Thierry Guerra. It is obvious, however, that Thierry has a personal historical past that could be hard to dispute considering he has recorded the whole thing on videotape. Although my assertion is that Thierry's alterative persona, Mister Brainwash, is a manipulated reality projected upon us. This makes him the link to Eisenstein's *Odessa Step Sequence* via the "carriage" in *Exit Through the Gift Shop*. This is not far-fetched, considering the genius prankster nature of Banksy, to suggest that spectacle of Mr. Brainwash is a social experiment pulled off by Banksy from behind a curtain. It is an experiment that entails bringing an artist out of nowhere, with no history at all and then placing this artist as the "name" responsible for a ridiculously appropriated and stupid body of work, already completely devoid of meaning, purpose, and content. Hype the artist through every means possible, projecting him to immediate social celebrity. At this point in the "drama" of the film all that is necessary for Bansky is to sit back and see who is willing to buy and for how much. All the while knowing that the art/ist is completely worthless.

91

While subtle, there is a fair amount of evidence to support this in *Exit Through the Gift Shop*, itself. Banksy certainly does not try to hide his contempt for Thierry Guetta, as an artist, in the film. He said something to the effect of that, after Thierry's instant fame, he [Banksy] doesn't really suggest to people, to make art anymore. He is also quoted in saying about the period after his *Barely Legal* show in Los Angeles,

"so then these famous auction houses... all of a sudden they were selling Street Art and everything was going a bit crazy... and suddenly it became all about the money... But it never was about the money. So I said to Thierry, right... you have the footage. You can tell the real story about what this is all about [referring to Street Art]. It's NOT about the hype. It's NOT about the money. Now is the time. You need to get your film out." [iv]

> **After seeing Thierry's film Banksy suggested that, "He [Thierry] might just be someone with mental problems that happened to have a camera."**
[v]

Seeing that Thierry's Street Art documentary wasn't going to make a statement about the origin or original purpose of Street Art, nor was it going to prove the ridiculousness of consumer culture in the Art World/Market, specifically in its relation with Street Art, Banksy decides to make his own project with this intent. Knowing the ephemeral nature of the street work and that there were years of footage lost, he devised a new plan to achieve this objective, of exposing the ridiculous nature of material consumerism. He does this by turning Thierry Guerra, someone with few, if any, intellectual qualities, into Mister Brainwash. Then he gives Mister Brainwash instant celebrity while documenting the whole process to turn into a film which holds a mirror on the face of consumer culture. The narrator explains:

"Thierry returned home to Los Angeles full of enthusiasm for his unexpected new assignment. Banksy just had given him, what he considered to be, a direct order, to put down his camera and become a Street Artist, himself" [vi]

There are a few things to be found in this statement. First and foremost, it identifies that it was Banksy's idea

that Thierry become a Street Artist. The second line is purposed to give the understanding that it was only a suggestion. But just because Thierry considered it to be a direct order, doesn't mean that it wasn't a direct order. This might be purely an argument of semantics, but it is important. The other thing that is important here is the necessity for Thierry to put down the video camera. Thierry needs to put the camera down so the truth is easier to manipulate. If he is constantly recording it leaves few gaps to insert false truth, or at least creates evidence against the false truth. Then suddenly and precisely at $00:52:00^{2}$ in the time code of *Exit Through the Gift Shop* Thierry is no longer the subject from behind the camera but the subject in front of the camera. But notice that the camera doesn't go away, it is still there with someone else holding it. It was someone who is steadier and more direct in focus/framing than Thierry had ever been. This leads the viewer to understand this cameraman had purpose and know how. In other words, he was a professional. Which raises the question who was paying for it, and why? Thierry, aka Mr. Brainwash, candidly provides further evidence to support this theory after he has broken his foot.

"It's like being an artist over night. I am a nobody. I never did an exhibition in a gallery really. I never show any work anywhere and I'm doing this big show, its all a... Its all a make-up kind of way." [vii]

Whatever the truth is, unless you are behind the curtain, you have no real knowledge of what is going on. This is the truth in both filmmaking and for the personas belonging to many Street Artists. In fact the only person who knows the historical truth of Banksy, is Banksy. The only one who can connect all the dots is Banksy. This puts him in a very powerful position, being that no one can fact check him. Knowing how little respect he has for authority, the powers that be, and his consistent mockery of consumerism, one must consider that Mr. Brainwash is a hoax fabricated by Banksy to exploit, discredit, and to expose the absurdity of the Art World/Market and culture that creates the commodity value of hype, fame, and celebrity.

One might never know if Banksy's greatest work is Mr. Brainwash himself or if he is challenging his audience to see through the hype of celebrity. Is he mocking the patrons of Mr. Brainwash, the trends of the contemporary art market and the art world in general? Is Mr. Brainwash, the celebrated failure of the revolution of Street Art, being used as a symbolic parallel to Potemkin's use in Eisenstein's film as the historical marker of the ultimate failure of the 1905 Russian Revolution? Is he testing our ability to find historical references? Is this piece in Chicago a clue to that fact? Or is the stencil a lie in itself, created to manipulate thoughts on reality in an effort to play both sides. Either way he has clearly separated himself from "Contemporary-POP," and the "Warholian" ideals of subtracting historical understanding from image and replacing it with the mindless material candy coating of celebrity, hype, and fame. In accepting his use of history as an aesthetic, one realizes he is not, as many in our culture do, using the blank mimicry of a recycled style. Instead, he has embodied revolutionary élan to leave the world with questions to consider. Regardless of his intent of the film I hope he will continue mocking the cultural logic of late capitalism that has led to the success of the subject of his film, and Thierry Guetta, aka Mr. Brainwash.

Is Banksy cheekily laughing at us all? Or is he leaving us "bread crumbs" to follow back to reason?

Footnotes:

1. This sentence originally read: "the spirit of the revolution soared over the Russian land." The word "Russian" was edited out to make the statement non-specific to the Russian revolution betrayed in Eisenstein's The Battleship Potemkin. This edit was made to allow the texted to elicit a emotional response from a broader audience, subtracted from the history associated with the Russian Revolution and the proceeding Communist establishment in Russia. This is an editorial trick Eisenstein is credited for developing.

2. Here might be the most direct evidence that this logic is sound. It is between the 00:51:47 – 00:52:22 seconds of The Battleship Potemkin that the baby in carriage is tumbling down the stairs.

CITATIONS:

i Sergei Eisenstein, The Battleship Potemkin, (Russian, 1925),Kino Video via Netflix.com, http://movies.netflix.com/WiPlayer?movieid=868691&trkid=2439677

ii Sergei Eisenstein, The Battleship Potemkin, (Russian, 1925),Kino Video via Netflix.com, http://movies.netflix.com/WiPlayer?movieid=868691&trkid=2439677

iii Sergei Eisenstein, The Battleship Potemkin, (Russian, 1925),Kino Video via Netflix.com, http://movies.netflix.com/WiPlayer?movieid=868691&trkid=2439677

iv *Exit Through the Gift Shop,* directed by Banksy (2010; United Kingdom: Paraniod Pictuers; distributed by Revolver Entertainment 2010), DVD

v *Exit Through the Gift Shop,* directed by Banksy (2010; United Kingdom: Paraniod Pictures; distributed by Revolver Entertainment 2010), DVD

vi *Exit Through the Gift Shop,* directed by Banksy (2010; United Kingdom: Paraniod Pictures; distributed by Revolver Entertainment 2010), DVD

vii *Exit Through the Gift Shop,* directed by Banksy (2010; United Kingdom: Paraniod Pictures; distributed by Revolver Entertainment 2010), DVD

Images:
Page 82
Artist: Banksy; Chicago, IL; 2010
Photographer: Thomas Fennell IV; 2010
Page 83
Stills from The Battleship Potemkin:
Sergei Eisenstein, *The Battleship Potemkin*, (Russian, 1925), from Kino Video via Netflix.com, *The Battleship Potemkin*, digital stills, 4 frames. WMDRM10 VIDEO, http://movies.netflix.com/WiPlayer?movieid=868691&trkid=2439677
Page 87
Artist: Banksy; Chicago, IL; 2010
Photographer: Thomas Fennell IV; 2010

"IS IT HIM? REALLY?"

The Moon's Teeth

Cast primal and bare in the reflections of the Sun
Stalking the night, exposing a sad truth
A beacon in the darkness
A beast in the moonlight

The shadow's reach grasps the landscape, guised in the night,
Mingling in forums recessed from light
Consumed by cannibalistic nature,
it digests the world's bile,
exposed in the fullness of the Lunatic Noctiluca.

Selene illuminates the earth, silhouetting the lustful hordes,
as a turbulent stillness expands in this restless mind,
fueling the veins of this pensive body,
only moments before it lashes out,
with rage and sorrow.

Against the wall of this cell
The structure of this world
The character of this being
And all others of fallible innocence.

Watch as this skin peels back,
along with this smile.
This face contorts,
revealing the undeniable truth,
of what is contained beneath a man beaten and worn
wide eyed to violent realities of this existence.

All the fatally explosive desires of futility,
only found in the broken heart of a volatile beast,
struggling to breathe.
I dare you, rattle my cage.
Be consumed by all that what once was a man.

-TIPTOE

Joseph J. Depre

In June of 2008 the Street Art Community of Chicago, and all of its extended "family", was rocked by the sudden passing of Brendan Scanlon better known through his omnipresent pseudonym SOLVE. SOLVE was one of the best known figures in the Chicago Street Art Community not only because of his prolific poster and sticker campaigns that slapped his name on nearly every available surface in Chicago or because of his innovative unconventional methods of "getting up." Instead, SOLVE was known as a galvanizing and positive charismatic presence that was unrelenting in championing the philosophy and importance of Street Art as a force that culturally enriched the artistic landscape of Chicago.

Like many others in the Chicago Street Art Community, I was lucky enough to call him my friend. He brought us all together and his loss was deeply felt. No longer could we witness the antics that made him so beloved to so many. Unique Street Art strategies, like designing "letters" detailing the more intimate depths of his thoughts then distributing those texts by leaving them in the street or dropping them in random mailboxes. Once, when he was on probation for his illegal Street Art activity, he installed a television on a CTA train reading, "we are experiencing legal difficulties…". Harmless, wondrous, funny and evocative artworks were the hallmark of this remarkable friend, advocate and beautiful "stranger."

The profound realization of all of our loss was made artistically evident by the way people marked his passing. Artists, many of them who were not regular practitioners of Street Art, immediately took to the street to create murals and Street Art installations in his honor. One of the most memorable of these was the spontaneous memorial shrine on Grand and Milwaukee. No one is quite sure how it started and as far as I know it was a completely unorganized effort. Contributions of art works and messages continued to appear for weeks from people who, of their own accord, came to show their respect. It was a truly beautiful thing in the wake of such a tragedy.

In the years after his death, those closest to him continue to keep Brendan in their hearts and on the street. Efforts have been continuous to produce and "get up" the "SOLVE" sticker with its unique font of Brendan's design. This labor of love has been taken to an unprecedented scale, one that includes nearly the entire globe. His stickers can be found on the streets of every continent; well, nearly all, as efforts to get up in Antarctica have proved difficult.

While I still deeply feel the lost of my friend, I am both awe struck and inspired by his continuous effect on those who knew him best. It is something beyond respect. It is love. A love that Brendan extended to all of those he knew and a love that united a community. May SOLVE's presence never die.

For those inspired to participate in keeping Brendon's spirit alive and present in the street, please go to SOLVESTICKERS.com

Thank you to all the photographers who made this book possible:
Oscar Arriola, Will Chambers, Juan "Angel" Chavez, Cyro, Chris Diers, Tom Fennell IV, The Grocer, Patritck Hershberger, Cody Hudson, MELT, Mental 312, Ray Noland, Brendan "SOLVE" Scanlon, Andy Schriver, Sighn, Elizabeth Slabaugh, The Viking, and You Are Beautiful
Without your generous efforts and your constant vigilance this project would not have seen fruition.

A Very Special Thank You to all of the artists working on the streets. Your work is an inspiration that beautifies life itself. **Thank You:**
Nick Adams, Artillery, Blütt, Bonus Saves, Hebru Brantley, Brooks Golden/The 7ist, Cdamage, Juan Chavez, Choke, CLS, Cody Hudson, CRO, Cyro, Don't Fret, 18 & Counting, 80 legs, Mike Genovese, Goons, The Grocer, Klepto Salem, Melt, Mental 312, Nice-One, Rejoice, Saro, Señor Codo, Sighn, Chris Silva, Chris Uphues, Solve, Sonny Rainclouds, Swiv, Tewz, Tiny, Tiptoe, Trampled, The Viking, You Are Beautiful, and all the others we have missed due to our limited knowledge.

Artist:
If one of your works has been featured in this here book and you would have preferred otherwise please contact us.
If your work has been displayed and credited improperly, you have our most sincere apology. Please let us know and we will make our best effort to correct the situation. While we have spent many hours walking the streets of Chicago, our knowledge is still very limited.
If you are a Chicago Street Artist and you feel like your work was overlooked, please let us know and we will do our best to represent you in any future editions. We meant no disrespect.
While we did our best to present all the artists respectfully and meant no harm with any of the work displayed, we acknowledge all difference of opinion and will try to respect any and all wishes from the Chicago Street Art Community.

Please Respect the Copyright:
All images submitted by the individual contributors have been offered with the understanding that they as originator retain copyright and are credited.
Chicago Street Art has been edited and designed by: Joseph J. Depre.
All essays have been written by:
Joseph J. Depre
Other words have been submitted from the artists: Bonus Saves, and Tiptoe
And the photographers: Oscar Arriola, Chris Diers, Thomas Fennell IV, and Patrick Hershberger
And are credited appropriately

Disclaimer:
All words relating to the art are solely the opinions of their authors and do not reflect the opinions of any of the Chicago Street Artists.

If you are a Chicago Street Artist and feel we have misrepresented your work, please contact us and let us know. We will do our best to correct the situation in any future editions.

The authors and contributors of this book in no way, shape, or form, approve of any action resulting in the destruction of property. We simply love the beauty of the creative spirit.

If you have looked through and read this book and are upset for any reason, please know this was not our intent. If you are really upset please seek medical attention.

If you have looked through and read this book and feel euphoric, know that we love you too!

Thank You
To the Chicago Urban Art Society
for allowing us to have our book release at your place.

Contact Information

You can contact the editor and publisher at the following email address:

ChicagoStreetArtBook @ Gmail.com

PLEASE let us know if you have any questions or concerns; We would love to hear your thoughts, especially if you liked it. Joseph J. Depre Editor and Publisher.

Artist Websites | Contact Information

PHOTOGRAPHERS:

Oscar Arriola
fotoflow@gmail.com
www.flickr.com/photos/fotoflow
www.fotoflow.blogspot.com

Chris Diers
ChrisDiers@gmail.com
photo website:
www.flickr.com/photos/senor_codo/
books website:
www.blurb.com/user/codo

Thomas Fennell IV
www.TEF4.com
Tom@TEF4.com

Patrick Hershberger
patrick.hershberger@gmail.com

Andrew Schriver
andrewjohn.zenfolio.com

ARTISTS:

Artillery
flickr.com/photos/cyanmizu/

BonusSaves
BonusSaves@yahoo.com
Flickr.com/bonusSaves

Brooks Golden
Brooksblairgolden.blogspot.com

Juan "Angel" Chavez
juanangelchavez.com

CRO
Creativerescue.org

Don't Fret
Dontfretart.com

80 Legs
AdieJanci@gmail.com
Seeingfromhearing.blogspot.com

The Grocer
Thegrocer.org
fresh@thegrocer.org

Klepto Salem
kleptosalem.tumblr.com/

MELT
flickr.com/toolbox

SARO
Artbysaro.com
artbysaro1@gamil.com

Brendan "SOLVE" Scanlon
solvesolvesolve.com
solvesfamily@solvelives.com

Señor Codo
Flickr.com/photos/senor_codo/

Sighn
Words@Sighn.net

Chris Silva
Chrissilva.com

Tiptoe
Tiptoe-studio.com

Tiny
tiny_stein@yahoo.com

YOU ARE BEAUTIFUL
you-are@you-are-beautiful.com

This project would not have been possible without constant support, guidance, and friendship from BonusSaves. Thanks buddy

Thank You

**Again and Again, Thank You!
I don't know what I would do without you...
You have my undying love...**

Credits

All images submitted by their respected contributors have been supplied on the understanding that they, as the originator, retain copyright and are credited.

Front Cover: **Artist**: Chris Sliva "Projections Delusions 2005" | **Photographer**: Chris Silva
Page 1: Acknowledgements
Page 2: Artist: Uknown | **Photographer:** Chris Diers **Page 3:** Dedication
Page 4: Words: Joseph J. Depre
Page 5: Words: Joseph J. Depre
     | **Artist:** Juan "Angel" Chavez - Mike Genovese - Cody Hudson; *Sur Del Cero*
     | **Photographer:** Cody Hudson.
Page 6 & 7: Artist: Juan "Angel" Chavez | **Photographer:** Juan "Angel" Chavez
Page 8 & 9: Artist: Mike Genovese | **Photographer:** Chris Diers.
Page 10: Artist: Cody Hudson | **Photographer:** from left: Chris Diers; Cody Hudson.
Page 11: Artist: Cody Hudson | **Photographer:** Will Chambers.
Page 12: Artist: Chris Silva | **Photographer:** Chris Silva.
Page 13: Artist: (Top: Chris Silva); (Bottom from Left: Chris Silva - David Cuesta - Mike Genovese; Chris Silva - Cody Hudson; Chris Silva - Cody Hudson; Chris Silva - David Cuesta)
     | **Photographer:** Chris Silva.
Page 14 & 15: Artist: BonusSaves | **Photographer:** Patrick Hershberger.
Page 16: Artist: Nice-One | **Photographer:** Chris Diers.
Page 17: Artist: Nice-One | **Photographer:** (Top from Left: Chris Diers; Chris Diers); (Bottom from Left: Thomas Fennell IV; Thomas Fennell IV)
Page 18: Artist: Brooks Golden/The Sevenist | **Photographer:** Thomas Fennell IV.
Page 19: Artist: Brooks Golden/The Sevenist | **Photographer:** Chris Diers.
Page 20: Artist: Don't Fret | **Photographer:** Thomas Fennell IV
Page 21: Artist: Don't Fret | **Photographer:** Chris Diers.
Page 22 & 23: Artist: Artillery | **Photographer:** Will Chambers.
Page 24: Artist: The Grocer | **Photographer:** The Grocer.
Page 25: Artist: The Grocer | **Photographer:** Thomas Fennell IV.
Page 26: Artist: Goons | **Photographer:** (Top from Left: Chris Deirs; Chris Diers; Oscar Arriola); (Middle from Left: Chris Deirs; Oscar Arriola); (Bottom from Left: Oscar Arriola; Chris Diers; Thomas Fennell IV)
Page 27: Artist: Goons | **Photographer:** Chris Diers.
Page 28: Artist: The Viking | **Photographer:** Oscar Arriola.
Page 29: Artist: (Top: The Viking); (Bottom: Goons and The Viking) | **Photographer:** (Top from left: The Viking; Chris Diers; Chris Diers); (Bottom from Left: Thomas Fennell IV; Thomas Fennell IV; Chris Diers)
Page 30: Artist: Sonny Rainclouds | **Photographer:** Patrick Hershberger.
Page 31: Artist: Sighn | **Photographer:** Sighn.
Page 32 & 33: Artist: You Are Beautiful | **Photographer:** You Are Beautiful.
Page 34: Artist: CLS | **Photographer:** Andrew Schriver.
Page 35: Artist: CLS | **Photographer:** Thomas Fennell IV.
Page 36: Artist: Tiny | **Photographer:** Patrick Hershberger.
Page 37: Artist: Hebru Brantley | **Photographer:** Chris Diers.
Page 38: Artist: MELT | **Photographer:** (Left: Oscar Arriola); (Right Top to Bottom: MELT; Chris Diers; MELT; MELT; MELT)
Page 39: Artist: CRO | **Photographer:** (Top from Left: Chris Diers; Anonymous Submission) (Middle from Left: Chris Diers, Anonymous Submission); (Bottom from Left: Thomas Fennell IV; Chris Diers)
Page 40: Artist: Choke | **Photographer:** (Top: Patrick Hershberger); (Bottom: Oscar Arriola)
Page 41: Artist: '18 & Counting' | **Photographer:** Chris Diers.
Page 42: Artist: Tewz | **Photographer:** Patrick Hershberger
Page 43: Artist: Crazy Talk/Artist Unkown | **Photographer:** (Top from Left: Patrick Hershberger; Patrick Hershberger); (Bottom from Left: Patrick Hershberger; Thomas Fennell IV.)
Page 44: Artist: CYRO | **Photographer:** (Left: Chris Diers); (Right Top to Bottom: CYRO)
Page 45: Artist: Party Patrol | **Photographer:** CYRO.

Page 46: Artist: Blütt | **Photographer:** Chris Diers.
Page 47: Artist: Artist Unknown | **Photographer:** Chris Diers.
Page 48: Artist: Rejoice | **Photographer:** Thomas Fennell IV;
Page 49: Artist: Rejoice | **Photographer:** (Left Top to Bottom: Chris Diers; Chris Diers; Chris Diers; Thomas Fennell IV.); (Right Top to Bottom: Chris Diers; Chris Diers; Chris Diers; Chris Diers.)
Page 50: Artist: SARO | **Photographer:** (top to Bottom) Patrick Hershberger; Chris Diers.
Page 51: Artist: SARO | **Photographer:** CYRO.
Page 52 & 53: Artist: Swiv | **Photographer:** Thomas Fennell IV.
Page 54 & 55: Artist: Klepto Salem | **Photographer:** Chris Diers.
Page 56 & 57: Artist: | **Photographer:** Thomas Fennell IV.
Page 58: Artist: Brendan "SOLVE" Scanlon | **Photographer:** Brendan "SOVLE" Scanlon.
Page 59: Artist: Brendan "SOLVE" Scanlon | **Photographer:** Oscar Arriola.
Page 60: Artist: MENTAL 312 | **Photographer:** (Top: MENTAL 312); (Bottom across: Thomas Fennell IV)
Page 61: Artist: MENTAL 312 | **Photographer:** Thomas Fennell IV
Page 62 & 63: Artist: SEÑOR CODO | **Photographer:** Chris Diers;
Page 64 & 65: Artist: TIPTOE | **Photographer:** Anonymous Submission.
Page 66: Artist: Nick Adams | **Photographer:** Thomas Fennell IV.
Page 67: Words: Joseph J. Depre | **Artist:** The BUFF | **Photographer:** Elizabeth Slabaugh.
Page 68: Words: BounsSaves | **Artist:** "It's Yours, Take It" | **Photographer:** Chris Diers
Page 69: Artist: BonusSaves; SEÑOR CODO | **Photographer:** Chris Diers
Page 70 & 71: Words: Thomas Fennell IV | **Artist:** Don't Fret | **Photographer:** Thomas Fennell IV.
Page 72: Words: Chris Diers | **Artist:** Nice-one | **Photographer:** Chris Diers.
Page 73: Words: Patrick Hershberger | **Artist:** Unknown Artist | **Photographer:** Patrick Hershberger
Page 74 & 75: Words: Oscar Arriola | **Artist:** Rejoice | **Photographer:** Oscar Arriola;
Page 76 & 77 Words: Joseph J. Depre | **Artist:** | **Photographer:** Anonymous Submission.
Page 78: Artist: Unknown Artist | **Photographer:** Chris Diers.
Page 79: Artist: Nice-one *"tribute to SOLVE"*;The Viking *"Blues"* | **Photographer:** Chris Diers.
Page 80 & 81: Words: Joseph J. Depre.
Page 82 & 83: Words: Joseph J. Depre | **Artist:** TIPTOE *The Heaviest Stone* | **Photographer:** Anonymous Submission
Page 84 & 85: Artist: TIPTOE *The Heaviest Stone* | **Photographer:** Anonymous Submission.
Page 86: Artist: Don't Fret | **Photographer:** Thomas Fenell IV
Page 87: Artist: Goons | **Photographer:** Thomas Fennell IV
Page 88: Words: Joseph J. Depre | **Artist:** Banksy | **Photographer:** Thomas Fennell IV.
Page 89: Words: Joseph J. Depre | **Artist:** Sergei Eisenstein, *"The Battleship Potemkin"* 1925 | **Photographer:** Stills from *The Battleship Potemkin* 1925;
Page 90: Words: Joseph J. Depre.
Page 91: Words: Joseph J. Depre.
Page 92: Words: Joseph J. Depre
Page 93: Words: Joseph J. Depre | **Artist:** Banksy; Unknown Artist | **Photographer:** Thomas Fennell IV
Page 94: Artist: Tiptoe "The Moon's Teeth" | **Photographer:** Anonymous Submission.
Page 95: Words: Tiptoe "The Moon's Teeth".
Page 96: Artist: Brendan "SOLVE" Scanlon remake | **Words:** Joseph J. Depre | **Photographer:** Anonymous Submission.
Page 97: Artist: BonusSaves, among others | **Words:** Joseph J. Depre | **Photographer:** Chris Diers.
Page 98 - 101: Credits
Page 102 & 103: Artist(s): Unknown | **Photographer:** Chris Diers
Page 104: Artists: (Top from Left: Unknown Artist; Rejoice; CRO); (Middle from Left: Ninja Girl; Charlie Owens; Trampled); (Bottom From Left: 80 Legs; Shift 2; Party Patrol) | **Photographer:** (Top from Left: Patrick Hershberger; Chris Diers; Thomas Fennell IV); (Middle from Left: Chris Diers; Oscar Arriola; Chris Diers); (Bottom from Left: 80 legs; Oscar Arriola; CYRO.)
Inside back cover: Artists: (Top from Left: Unknown Artist; Sonny Rainclouds; Senor CODO); (Middle from Left: TEWZ; Chris Uphues "heart" and Risk "hands";); (Bottom from Left: Brendan "SOLVE" Scanlon; Jim Cereal; Unknown Artist.) | **Photograper:** (Top from Left: Chris Diers; Chris Diers; Chris Diers); (Middle From Left: Chris Diers; Chris Diers: Thomas Fennell IV); (Bottom from Left: Chris Diers; Thomas Fennell IV; Thomas Fennell IV.)
Back Cover: Artists: (Top from Left: Nice-One; Chris Silva – Mike Genovese; Brendan "SOLVE" Scanlon); (Middle from Left: BonusSaves; Juan "Angel" Chavez; Klepto Salem); (Bottom from Left: Goons; TIPTOE; Unknown Artist.) | **Photograper:** (Top from Left: Thomas Fennell IV; Chris Silva; Chris Diers); (Middle from left: Chris Diers; Juan "Angel" Chavez; Chris Diers); (Bottom from Left: Thomas Fennell IV; Anonymous Submission; Thomas Fennell IV)

IF YOU STEP IN THE RING,
EXPECT TO GET HIT.

chi